"I didn't think there w[...]
how to have a quiet time [...]
30 Ways to Wak[...]
I couldn't put it dow[...]
practical applications and [...]
she gives advice and stimul[...]g [...] that bring new life
and vitality to spending time alone with God.
Throughout the book Pam adds extraordinary ideas for
getting children excited about the Bible too.
Pam's unique insights will permanently make
my quiet time more meaningful."

CAROL KENT, *speaker, author and president of*
Speak Up Speaker Services

———

"Excellent. Refreshing. Insightful. My quiet times will
never be the same after reading Pam's creative ideas
for keeping your love relationship with God alive."

PAT CLARY, *president, Women's Ministries Institute*

———

"Do you want to connect with God but nothing you do
seems to bridge the gap you feel? This book will give you great,
fresh new ideas for making your quiet time
the meaningful experience with the Savior you are seeking."

ROBANNE BURNS, *Forest Home Christian Conference Center*

———

"If you are looking to freshen your relationship with God,
then you will love this book. Pam Farrel has written
an inspiring book packed full with creative ideas
for connecting with God in the day to day.
I've read a lot of books on quiet times
but have never come across so many new ideas
for drawing closer to God's heart."

SHELLY ESSER, *editor of* Just Between Us *magazine*

———

"In the rich tradition of finding God in the ordinary,
Pam shows us how to pull objects and activities out of everyday
life and make them a part of our quiet time.
In this way our quiet time is no longer a burdensome chore
but a moment with the One who loves us."

JAN JOHNSON, *author of* Enjoying the Presence of God *and*
Living a Purpose-Full Life

30 Ways to WAKE UP YOUR QUIET TIME!

Pam Farrel

InterVarsity Press
Downers Grove, Illinois

InterVarsity Press
P.O. Box 1400, Downers Grove, IL 60515
World Wide Web: www.ivpress.com
E-mail: mail@ivpress.com

InterVarsity Press® is the book-publishing division of InterVarsity Christian Fellowship/USA®, a student movement active on campus at hundreds of universities, colleges and schools of nursing in the United States of America, and a member movement of the International Fellowship of Evangelical Students. For information about local and regional activities, write Public Relations Dept., InterVarsity Christian Fellowship/USA, 6400 Schroeder Rd., P.O. Box 7895, Madison, WI 53707-7895.

All Scripture quotations, unless otherwise indicated, are taken from the Holy Bible, New International Version®. NIV®. Copyright ©1973, 1978, 1984 by International Bible Society. Used by permission of Zondervan Publishing House. All rights reserved.

On page 42 the lyrics to "You Are the Rock of My Salvation" are by Teresa Muller, ©1982 by Maranatha Music, used by permission.

Cover illustration: Roberta Polfus

ISBN 0-8308-1128-1

Printed in the United States of America ∞

Library of Congress Cataloging-in-Publication Data

Farrel, Pam, 1959-

   30 ways to wake up your quiet time / Pam Farrel.
     p. cm.
   ISBN 0-8308-1128-1 (alk. paper)
   1. Spiritual life—Christianity.   2. Prayer—Christianity.
 I. Title.
 BV4501.2.F325   1999
 248.3—dc21

                                      99-15062
                                          CIP

15	14	13	12	11	10	9	8	7	6	5	4	3	2	1

11	10	09	08	07	06	05	04	03	02	01	00	99

To the congregations
of Calvary Bible Church
and Valley Bible Church,
and to all the wonderful
organizations and churches
that have invited
Bill and me to speak.
Thank you!
Service is a great
catalyst for creativity.
The teacher always gets more
out of a lesson than
the students.

Contents

Introduction
Time to Wake Up

My husband, Bill, and I enjoyed the movie *Groundhog Day* in which Bill Murray woke up every morning to live February 2 over and over again. At first Bill Murray desperately wanted to escape from this routine, but then he began to be more creative with it, and the routine began to help him grow and mature as a person. He learned what priorities were, how to be more loving, how to treat people right. A routine of daily time with God can be the same way, in the routine we can either lose hope, zest and creativity or we can use the routine as a framework for our lives. As we creatively spend time with God, God becomes more real.

When my son Brock was about two, my husband and I led a youth leaders' retreat together. While I was leading the group at one point, the babysitter came to pull Bill out of the back row. It seems that Brock had some questions that he wanted answered right then.

Brock sat and asked all kinds of spiritual questions like: "Where did God come from? How did bad get here? Why do you teach big people the Bible?" Finally, Bill thought this was some big spiritual teachable moment so he asked Brock if he wanted to ask Jesus into his heart.

Being a first-time dad, he didn't realize that this question might be a little premature. But Brock handled it well. Brock said, "No, Dad, when Jesus gets out of the Bible, then I'll ask him into my life." And that is the task at hand, to make the words of the Bible so real that Jesus isn't some flannelboard God but the intimate Savior, the indwelling Holy Spirit and the caring always-present Father.

Tools for Growth

I want to experience God with the range of emotions that he created me with. I want to see him work in a variety of settings to conform me to his image, so I want to give him lots of opportunities and lots of tools.

My dad was in equipment service for a large farm machinery company. I used to be so amazed when people would call him on the phone and he could tell them exactly what tool to pull off the shelf and exactly where to turn, push, pull or tweak some part. It seemed that he had the machines totally memorized and all the parts and all the tools readily accessible. Our garage was lined with ten-drawer toolboxes, every wall was covered in pegboard and organized with just the right tool for any job. I also want to have a garage full of tools so I can capture as many facets as possible of the amazing God I serve.

This book is dedicated to fellow travelers who long to respond to God, to be attentive to his voice. You can use this in a variety of ways: to accompany your normal daily routine to provide a change of pace, to add in a new idea to your quiet times once a week or to use for thirty days in a row.

These ideas are designed to counteract dryness or boredom, to provide relational connectedness if your quiet times have become academic or intellectual exercises or just to allow you to have a little fun and enjoy the presence of the One who created you. The ideas here are meant to spark your own ideas. Picture them as spiritual caffeine for the soul. Pour a big cup and drink your fill.

Others have: Charles Dickens heartily recommends the New Testament as "the very best book that ever was or ever will be written." General Douglas MacArthur committed his schedule to it: "Never a night goes by, be I ever so tired, but I read the Word of God before I go to bed." George Washington said, "It is impossible to rightly govern the world without God and the Bible." And other presidents echo this sentiment. Abraham Lincoln said, "The Bible is the best gift God has ever given to man." Dwight D. Eisenhower agreed: "To read the Bible is to take a trip to a fair land where the spirit is strengthened and faith renewed."

Warning: The Bible is habit-forming. Regular use causes loss of anxiety, decreased appetite for lying, cheating, stealing and hating. Symptoms: increased sensations of love, peace, joy, compassion.

1.

JESUS HAD A
QUIET TIME

So have you ever wondered why we're supposed to have a quiet time with God anyway? Be honest—for some of us it was simply because we were told that it is the right thing to do. But why is it the right thing to do? I like to look at Christ's life to find the reasons.

It's instructional. We know that Jesus spent a lot of time with the Scriptures because when Jesus went to the temple at twelve, his conversations with and questions of the rabbis left them in amazement (Luke 2:41-47). In the same way, daily time in the Word is like our physical skeleton, it is the framework on which our whole life is built.

It's relational. Before Jesus launched his ministry, he went into the desert for a forty-day fast—to discipline his heart to hear the voice of the Father. That's why he knew exactly how to handle Satan's temptations (Luke 4:1-13). Before he chose the Twelve, Jesus prayed all night (Luke

6:12-13). When the crowds pressed in, he found a quiet place to get away and pray (Mark 1:32-35). Before he went to the cross, he went to the garden to pray (Mark 14:32-42). Like Jesus we need to communicate with the Father continually, especially in times of stress.

It's powerful. After the disciples spent time with Jesus, he sent them out two by two, and they were given amazing power by God to heal the sick, the deformed and the dismayed (Mark 6:12-13). Jesus prayed in a solitary place before that little boy's lunch turned into a feast for five thousand (Mark 6:30-44). He prayed at Lazarus' tomb—a commanding "Come forth!" (John 11:41-43) He even prayed from the cross, "Father, into your hands I commit my spirit" (Luke 23:46). Spending time with God accomplishes much.

Make the Connection

What motivates you to spend time with God? Jesus wanted a connection. Before all the big moments of his earthly life, he connected to the Father. Spend some quiet times looking up the passages cited from Jesus' life to get a picture of how he spend time with God.

Why have you been having a quiet time? Christian duty? guilt? bragging rights? to gain an air of spiritual superiority? to wow people with your Bible memory skills?

If you have been laboring under a false motivation, ask God to help you refocus your quiet times on connecting with him.

2.

THE HEART OF
A CHILD

Jesus said, "Blessed are the children." He wants us to
approach him with the heart of a child.

When I was eight years old, I memorized the Twenty-
Third Psalm, and my reward was a small white cross on a
beautiful purple cord. And on it was printed, "He is risen."
At night that cross would glow in the dark in my room. As
I listened to my parents arguing because of my father's
drinking, that cross became a beacon of hope to me.

Get into the Mind and Heart of a Child

*Connect your relationship with God to a symbol of hope from
your childhood or early adulthood.* Did you fall asleep with a
stuffed animal, a music tape or other comforting item?
Maybe there is something that you could place on your
key ring or in a frame in your hallway or sit on your desk
that could remind you that God is always there, a very
present help in times of need (Psalm 46:1).

Try praying like a child. Pray *Now I lay me down to sleep, I pray the Lord my soul to keep . . .* , then talk to God about how you'd like him to keep your heart and soul.

Pick up a children's devotional or Bible, a Vacation Bible School or Sunday-school leader's guide and incorporate some of the activities into your quiet time. You could try coloring a Sunday-school take-home paper, singing children's choruses or even making a craft! (Every time I smell Ivory soap, I think of the "Bible" I carved out of a bar at VBS when I was ten!) Children's Bible storybooks can provide a fresh viewpoint especially on devotional topics dealing with lying, sharing and whining—all issues this heart of mine still struggles with.

Have a quiet time with a child. Ask the child to teach you and explain to you what they think a verse means. Recently, after my husband Bill had waxed eloquent one Sunday morning, I asked our eight-year-old son what he learned from Daddy's sermon. Waiting for the typical, "Jesus loves me" answer, I was pleasantly surprised when he said, "You shouldn't make up excuses not to obey God." Wow!

If you try some of these ideas in your quiet time, you might be surprised to find that as you gain the heart of a child, you feel younger in the process!

3.

DEAR JESUS

When I was a college student, I went to a Campus Crusade leadership conference. I had recently rededicated my life to Christ, and I was zealously devouring one Bible study guide after another. It was almost like my goal was to complete as many books as possible—like I was earning merit badges by completing them.

During one small group discussion the leader asked us about our quiet times. As we were finishing the talk, the leader said: "Oh, you might want to buy a journal. I write letters to Jesus after I have read a passage in the Bible. I write down my feelings, what I've learned, what I'd like to learn—things like that. It's on my bed, and you can look at it if you'd like." Then she left the room.

Look at it! Of course we wanted to look at it. It was like an open invitation to read someone's diary! But instead of a catalog of daily news like, "Today, I saw John," I got a glimpse into a real relationship between God and a college senior—and I wanted that kind of relationship. I went right downstairs to the bookstore and bought a beautiful clothbound journal filled with empty pages just waiting to be filled.

See How You've Grown

My journal became a place to write out my thoughts, to think through the decisions of my life. Catherine Calvert wrote of the benefits of solitary reflection in *Victoria:* "In solitude we heard our own footsteps walking into the future."

Recently I came across my quiet-time journal from years ago. I noted an entry just days before my wedding was to take place. My mother-in-law-to-be had just dropped the news that she wasn't going to attend our wedding. The journal held my sadness. Writing brought me to a place of acceptance, then to a place where I could pray for her in compassion.

On the pages before and right after our wedding I saw pieces of sentences that described the woman I wanted God to make me and the kind of marriage I wanted to have: *Help me be extra understanding of others. Help me see their needs, not just my own. . . . Please give Bill and me the character qualities we'll need. Make us useable . . . give us ideas that glorify you. . . . Let us be an example. . . .* The more I read, the more I realized that God had answered my prayers. God had made me into the woman I longed to become, one day at a time.

What Should I Write?

If you are having trouble knowing what to write in a journal, try answering some of the following questions.

☐ What does this verse say?

☐ How does it apply to me?
☐ How can I apply it today?
☐ Do I know someone else that needs this message?
☐ How do I feel about what I've read?
☐ What do I feel about my life?
☐ What are my hopes and dreams?
☐ What are my expectations of God? Are they biblical?
☐ Is there something I can learn from this Bible character?

At an "Oasis" retreat designed to teach women how to spend extended times with God, I received this advice.

> Calm your mind, relax your body, move in faith to receive what Jesus will reveal to you. Read the passage slowly and gently until you come to a word or phrase that makes an impression on your mind or an impact on your heart. Reflect on that thought, inviting it to be a guest in your heart. Ask the Lord any questions you may have about the passage. Listen with your heart to what he says. . . . Write about the experience . . . create a poem . . . draw a picture . . . compose a psalm of praise.

At one of the Oasis conferences, I remember the encouragement to close down the windows of responsibility of my life just like we close down the windows on our computer programs. As I slow down, clicking the mouse of my life to off, I then find I have better reception to what God is saying. Sometimes I do this by freewriting in my journal, logging random thoughts as they enter my mind. I record turns of phrases, poems or emotions as I need to release them from the confines of my heart. I find that if I close down my frenzied activity, I have much I want to journal back to him!

4.

HE MAKES ME FEEL
LIKE DANCING!

Dance was David's response to victory. Dance was Miriam's response to the parting of the Red Sea. She led hundreds in a cheer for joy. Dance can be a meaningful part of your quiet times as you express your feelings to God.

I was reared to dance. Years of classical ballet training in pink tights and a black leotard doing pliés turned into years as a gymnast creating competitive routines. My grandparents and parents danced the classic ballroom waltzes, swing and others on our linoleum floor. My memories are of me in my flannel jammies and my dad or grandfather all dressed up and headed out for a night of toe tapping.

I've always been comfortable expressing my feelings through dance—but it hasn't always been spiritually meaningful. That only happened as I did a study of Scripture and discovered that God intended dance to be used as a part of worship. The book of Psalms particularly reveals that he knew we needed to respond not just intellectually to his greatness and majesty; we needed to respond physically as well.

> You turned my wailing into dancing;
>> you removed my sackcloth and clothed me with joy,
> that my heart may sing to you and not be silent. (Psalm 30:11-12)

> Let them praise his name with dancing
>> and make music to him with tambourine and harp.
> For the LORD takes delight in his people. (Psalm 149:3-4)

I took a Jewish folk-dance class and the holiness of dance became real to me. As the teacher explained the meaning of the names of the dances and their steps, I began to grasp the full picture of God's plan. One dance had a step for water, and the instructor went on and on about how important water was to Israel. I thought about how Jesus said, "I am the living water."

At the moment my feet were moving to the music and doing the steps that meant water, I knew that for me the living water is what I need for survival. And it is what everyone in Israel and everywhere else needs for survival. I had intellectually known that for years and years, but in that moment my whole body could respond to the truth of that one simple phrase of Scripture. Though my hands were clasped and raised in the circle of dancers, my heart was bowed in reverent worship.

Get Moving

A variation of a dance quiet time can be an aerobic

workout to Christian music, a Christian music video or one of the Christian aerobic workout tapes. These tools offer basic training so that you can learn to move your body again if it's been awhile!

While speaking at a retreat in Vancouver, Washington, I enjoyed an afternoon of aerobic movement called *Innergize*. It was a wonderful mix of upbeat praise music and quiet, contemplative movement and music. There were times when I could simply close my eyes and meditate on God's goodness toward me. Because of my background in dance and gymnastics, my feet and body simply joined in the celebration. During the quiet stretching time, I could review and reevaluate my life while I prayed to God over my concerns.

Professional counselor Earl Henslin says that often it is after intense exercise and rest that our minds think clearest. I also have seen that I am most creative after I have exercised and prayed. It is as if those two activities serve as the eraser on the chalkboard of my life, wiping away the superfluous noise of busyness.

Satan loves to distort God's good gifts. Sex is a God-given gift that has been distorted by misuse. Music can be distorted to move people away from God rather than to him. And in the same way dance has been misused by many (see the story of Herod's daughter in Mark 6:17-29) to allure and seduce. So the church has run away from the gift instead of redeeming it and giving it a respectable place as a response of heart to the vast wonderfulness of God.

When we attend sporting events, the thousands present think nothing of jumping to their feet and whooping out a cheer at a touchdown or homerun. God is better than any home run or touchdown, and our body longs to jump to our feet and cheer his majesty. Dance is a tool God provided to allow us an expression of exuberant thankfulness.

"If you're happy and you know it, tap your toes!"

5.

HEART OF DARKNESS

In the movie *Star Wars* one of the most intense scenes is when Luke Skywalker discovers his own father had defected to the dark side. The audience is gripping their seats when Darth Vader then tries to recruit Luke to the dark side. In real life, the intense battle is the same. Overcoming our past or our dark side can be so difficult. All of us know all too well those areas that are less than perfect in our own life. Often we are acutely aware of just how far we fall short of God's plan for us.

Too often we try to bury our dark side, hoping somehow it will just magically disappear, but it doesn't. Just like leftovers in the refrigerator left unattended, the bacteria spreads and consumes a once-tasty dish. When we are feeling overwhelmed by the grip of terror and darkness on our hearts, we need to spend some quiet times focused on overcoming our dark side.

Steps to Victory

In our church part of the counseling process is working through *Steps to Freedom in Christ* by Neil Anderson. When a person goes through the seven steps in that book, all their emotional and spiritual footholds are openly laid out just like playing cards out for a game of solitaire. Basically, this book helps us learn what things have or could trip us up in trying to be all God created us to be.

To win a victory over the dark side, we must be very deliberate. Make a list of weaknesses, then go to the Bible to find verses to equalize your life.

Carol was an older woman who had made some major marital and mothering mistakes by abandoning her marriage and children. After coming to Christ she still felt frozen in her personal growth. As she listed her weaknesses, it became apparent that she had done well in memorizing verses about God's grace, but she'd failed to take the next step. She needed to integrate verses that could fortify her heart, strengthening her for the journey.

Carol's list of weaknesses included fear, feeling inadequate, feeling stupid, feeling overwhelmed by the most simple schedule and so on. Next to each weakness she listed traits of God that can counter the weakness. For example, next to "stupid" she wrote "all-knowing mind of Christ." Next to "overwhelmed" she wrote "able." Next to "inadequate and spineless" (she was hard on herself) she wrote "adequate, strong, fortress." By using a good concordance she located verses that included those key words. She chose her favorite ten, wrote them on a computer in a pretty font, personalized the verses, then printed it on beautiful paper and framed it.

Sheryl, another woman wanting to shrink her dark side down, had no contact with her real father growing up and had a series of abusive stepdads. Sheryl wrote out a set of verses that described God as a father. In her hallway hangs this set of verses with some artwork depicting God in a fatherly manner.

Lisa had too often chosen unhealthy men to somehow sweep into her life and rescue her, but instead they would just hurt her and use her. Lisa wrote out a set of verses that described God as her prince and king, and herself as a chosen daughter of the King. This exercise was a turning point for Lisa. Those verses helped her heal from a bitter divorce, set new dating standards, keep those standards, marry a wonderful godly man and establish a ministry to other single mothers.

You can create your own devotional of verses by topic to address your dark side. Resources that group verses by topic are *Nave's Topical Bible* and *Daily Light for the Daily Path,* which is simply a collection of similar verses with a morning and evening reading selection. A good concordance will also be a handy resource in locating verses for specific areas of concern.

When I find verses that address my dark side, I turn them into bookmarks. I laminate them and make a magnet for my refrigerator or office. I post them on brightly colored paper on my bathroom mirror. Or I frame them. Then, when those thorn-in-the-flesh days hit, I have the resources to combat them readily at hand. I have found that by investing time in my quiet times to locate these special verses, those dark days, those dismal depressing days, and those days that feel like life is sitting on your chest happen less and less often.

Dealing with Lingering Guilt

If you have confessed your sin and have tried to deal with those nagging dark-side issues but a skeleton in your closet keeps clanking its noisy chain and making you feel guilty, get it out with the following exercise.

Write all those nagging sins down, then write the test of 1 John 1:9 over it—right over the top, ink over ink! *If we confess our sins, he who is faithful and just will forgive us our sins and cleanse us from all unrighteousness.* This creates a picture of how God blots out sin. You may then want to destroy the list. (A fireplace can come in handy here.) It is such a relief to see that all our ugly thoughts and selfish actions are creatively cremated by God's powerful love.

Tired of living in depressing darkness? To gain freedom, let his light shine in the dark places of your life today.

6.

CREATING A
LEGACY

In junior high I ran on a relay team in track. **Exhilaration** catapulted me forward in the race as the baton was successfully slapped into my hand. I was momentarily overjoyed with the responsibility for racing it down the track and entrusting it to the next runner. The relay race gave four of us the opportunity to do more together than we could ever do on our own.

The purpose of spending time with God is not just for your growth and peace. Your relationship with God is a relay race that builds a family legacy.

Make Your Faith a Gift

Try reading the Bible through and marking it up to give as a gift to a teen or young adult. Point out the verses that you think would encourage or strengthen your sons or daughters, godchildren, nieces or nephews, or grand-children by highlighting, underlining and writing notes in the margin.

Recall the verses that helped you choose a career, commit to your mate or navigate a significant transition in your life. I like to use markings for these verses to encourage dialogue. For my sons I highlight some of my favorite verses and write in the margin: *This helped me decide to marry your dad—ask me about it. I was going through a very hard time and this verse pulled me through, ask me why.* I have also pointed out their father's favorite verses. And I mark passages that have inspired other leaders who have captured the respect of each of my sons. I also made sure I marked the verses that are a part of our family's mission statement so they could get a sense of God's calling in our lives.

This gift Bible you are preparing is a great opportunity to train your son or daughter in some Bible study skills. In the margin, you can write activities or suggest studies you want your child to engage in. In Brock's Bible I have encouraged him to title each Psalm. I have asked him to do a character study in the book of Daniel, suggesting ways he could mark verses that showed positive character qualities in Daniel's life. I titled each chapter in the book of Ruth.

Chapter 1: Excellent Statement (Can you find and underline the key verses in this chapter, Brock?)

Chapter 2: Excellent Woman (Mark each place that shows how and why Ruth was such a great woman.)

Chapter 3: Excellent Plan (Brock, look up the culture of Israel during this time in a Bible dictionary or commentary [I suggested several resources]. How does knowing the background and culture help you understand why Naomi had a good plan in sending Ruth to Boaz at the threshing floor?)

Chapter 4: Excellent Man (What is Boaz doing here and how does this show he was a good, trustworthy man ready for the responsibility of marriage?)

At the end I wrote: Excellent Ending (What does this show you about seeking after and following God's will?)

At the front of each of my sons' Bibles I have written quotes under a variety of headings: "Mommilies," things I always say; "Dad Talk," quotes and pet phrases from Bill; "Other Great Quotes," which include thoughts from famous people about the importance of the Bible in everyday life.

On the flyleaf of Brock's Bible, I wrote a personal inscription that includes a story I heard told about Anne Graham Lotz, daughter of Billy Graham. There was a time in Anne's youth when she was struggling with her faith and a wise youth leader said to her, "You have been looking at God through a prism; your mom's, your dad's and the church's expectations color your view of God. Look at God for yourself. Go on with God."

In the flyleaf of Zachery's Bible I have recently written headings such as "Trust Your Abilities," "Keep God's Priorities," "Keep Your Word," "Have Courage," "Make Decisions," each with a set of verses I found helpful in those areas.

Make It an Event
When presenting this gift, make it memorable. You might take the young person to a favorite chapel or camp where a special choice was made in your own life. Present

the gift on an important birthday or as a marker for a special event. The Bible might also be given in conjunction with another gift that symbolizes a marker in his or her life. For example, it could accompany a purity ring, a set of car keys or "something old, something new, something borrowed or something blue."

You might even want to create a special worship service for the event. A special family devotional time in a special location would give a tangible way to celebrate the significance of the event. This can be a wonderful gift at a time in life when young people want to stand on their own. They are seeking autonomy and this is a way of saying, "You are an adult now. All my advice and, more importantly, all God's advice is in here. I trust you to use it to discern and live out God's will for your life."

As I read the Bible through for my three sons (one Bible for each son), I gained a new appreciation for Scripture. I valued my own time in the Word more because not only was I growing as an individual, I was building a legacy. Strengthen their grip and you'll find your own is stronger for it.

7.

POSITION
YOURSELF

Author and editor John Duckworth was in need of a way
to reconnect with God that would help him adjust to the
tension of trying to represent God while living in a highly
competitive world.

I sat on the couch and bowed my head. But for some
reason I couldn't pray. My position was wrong, I thought.
I'd been thinking of myself more highly than I should,
and now I needed to be lower. I kneeled, I couldn't recall
the last time I'd done that, but I tried it now. It didn't feel
right either. I needed to be lower still. The only other
position I could think of was bowing down like Muslims
did when they faced Mecca. Too strange, I thought. I
never prayed that way, I couldn't.

Yet a moment later I found myself on the floor, down
on my face, my forehead to the carpet. Finally it felt right.
I started to pray silently, but stopped. It didn't seem to be
a time to talk, but to listen. I waited for a long time, and

a verse I'd known for years whispered in my memory: Be still and know that I am God. (Ps. 46:10) . . . I just wanted to be still and know God.

I wanted it so much that the next morning I got up half an hour early and bowed down on the floor again. And the next morning, and the next. I didn't even bring a Bible with me at first. I just cleared my mind and thought about that verse. Soon I found myself wanting to worship this God who was so high above me. I would talk to him a little or think about a hymn. But mostly I was still. . . . A month of mornings became two, then three. Then six months passed, and a year. But it was no achievement. It was eating because I was hungry. It was forgetting the rules and making it up as I went along. It was one of the easiest things I'd ever done. (As quoted by Jan Johnson in *Enjoying the Presence of God*)

Pray in a New Position

Praying in a position that is not the norm for you can change your heart, not just your body position.

When I am really upset, lifting my hands straight over my head like an Olympic weightlifter helps me. I simply pray, "Here it is. I can't carry it anymore. It's yours!"

A friend of mine, when she feels like she is whining in prayer, puts her hand out like a traffic officer halting a stream of angry honking cars and says to herself, "Don't go there. Let it go."

Richard Foster settles into solitude by using a "palms up, palms down," approach. He places his palms down to show that he is giving his burdens to God. Then he turns his palms up to show that he is ready to receive from God. (Taken from Jan Johnson in *Enjoying the Presence of God.*)

After being in ministry with my husband for a few years, I found myself moved by a sermon I listened to on tape. In a state of exhaustion the pastor was up late at night talking to God about his growing sense of frustration with his church. The more he talked to God, the more he sensed God telling him that he was too proud. He knelt by the dining-table chair, and then he just fell on the floor begging God to do something with him and with the church. As I listened, I suddenly felt free to be myself. I knew I had felt like falling down on my face, crying over some of the things I faced. Somehow knowing that someone I respected ended up on the floor under his kitchen table in despair gave me permission to be more real when I prayed too.

If someone were to have a camera on me when I prayed, they'd see I am very animated because I now talk to God with more of my personality. I move when I pray. I pace. I kneel. Then I sprawl out face to the floor or fling myself across my bed and pour out my heart before heaven. I have noticed a pattern—the more important the topic, the more animated I become or the lower I prostrate myself before his throne. For me, changing positions is a tangible way to signal my heart that it is time to soften and yield.

It is common for psalmist to call people to "bow down . . . and kneel before the LORD" (Psalm 95:6), "walk before the LORD" (Psalm 116:9) and "stand in his holy place" (Psalm 24:3-4). In the same way, physical change will bring spiritual renewal for you.

8.

THINK ON THIS!

Some days are just the pits! Bad news looms overhead.
Fears overwhelm. Frustrations consume our minds.
What can break the downward spiral of negativity?

Philippians 4:8 says, "Whatever is true, whatever is
noble, whatever is right, whatever is pure, whatever is
lovely, whatever is admirable—if anything is excellent or
praiseworthy—think about such things." When you are
down, spend your quiet time thinking of things that are
lovely, like a rose, a ballet dancer or a crystal vase. Think
of excellent things: a touchdown, an A paper, a promo-
tion or raise in rank. Creating your own list of things to
remember when you are tempted to complain or think
impure, unkind or just plain ugly thoughts. Post the list
in a place that you are often grumpy, like in the car you
commute in, above the washer and dryer or kitchen sink.

To take this quiet time a step further, create a Philippians 4:8 photo album. Put personal photos of the people, places and things you love most in a scrapbook. In
colorful markers, write out favorite verses to accompany

these candid shots. You will find this book an encouragement in times of discouragement and depression.

This quiet time can also help those who are struggling to overcome a negative habit. Having a ready list of positive words helped a friend kick a cussing habit. Many in our ministry have been helped to kick addictive behaviors because they have a list of things they can do instead of shopping, drinking, gambling or drugs.

Sometimes this activity can help those in relationship crisis. A newly divorced woman wrote out a list of safe people and places to go instead of bars. She even took it one step further and made a file of places she'd like to vacation at or travel to. Things she'd like to do in her new life. Even though she was brokenhearted over her husband's affair and the impending divorce, this list helped her and her children as it moved them forward into new positive experiences and memories.

Early in my Christian experience I was encouraged to have a specific place to meet God daily. I try to create an oasis where I can settle my heart. A positive place meant I would look forward to going and meeting God there. A favorite rocker, window seat, patio chair or other comfortable spot can become a Philippians 4:8 place that can cause a change of attitude.

Find a way to allow your favorite things to encourage you.

9.

HE WALKS WITH ME & HE TALKS WITH ME

When my father died, traditional quiet times were not easing the pain. My friend Gail brought over a gift from my women's ministry team. It was a small rose bush. Planting, pruning and caring for that plant gave me time to talk to God about my feelings and a positive result—a living, growing, blooming beautiful result. It felt like my dad's death wasn't insignificant but rather significant because one small corner of the world became a more beautiful place, a reminder of a life lived.

Commemorating Significant Events

There are many significant events and transitions in our lives when a traditional Bible-study quiet time just doesn't seem to fit.

☐ Our engagement was celebrated on the beach as we

stood and prayed together, watching the waves crash over the rocks and splash over our toes.

☐ The day of my wedding, my best friend came over early in the morning, and we went for a prayer walk in the park around the corner.

☐ When Bill and I were trying to decide our future and were wondering if God was calling us out of youth ministry and into the senior pastorate, we sat and sang praises at the edge of a beautiful lake, then we prayed.

☐ Nearly every year our family makes a trek up a mountain to a little chapel, and we each leave our prayer requests for the coming year at the foot of a rough hewn cross.

☐ Sunrise on the Kilaea river in Hawaii in a kayak was a wonderful way for Bill and me to recommit our marriage and ministry to God.

Some days just demand that we stop, step out of the normal pace of life and look full face into the creation so we can connect with the Creator. Of course, you can pray in your dining room at home, but somehow when pivotal prayers are uttered in poignant settings they become etched in your mind and heart. Look at the calendar for the coming year, is there an event you can make special by stepping into nature and feeding your relationship with God?

Reconnecting with the Creator

You may want to take up a hobby that will take you out of the city and back to nature so you can slow your pace and enjoy creation—and the presence of God. Backpacking, hiking, mountain climbing, kayaking, sailing and birdwatching are a few ways to reconnect to nature.

The psalms record David's connection with the Creator through creation. Psalm 19:1 says, "The heavens declare the glory of God; the skies proclaim the work of his hands." There are days that I long for a meaningful connection with the Creator, in his creation. Emotional pressure seems to drive me outdoors, for a breath of fresh air.

During the period after my father's death, I felt the pressures of my life escalating exponentially: deadline upon deadline, medical problems, grief and mounting legal responsibilities as my father's executor, unwarranted criticism of our ministry, huge situations crying out for solutions, plus the daily stress of leading the church, my own ministry and my family. I sat in my doctor's office in tears. All I wanted to do was escape and drive to the beach and spend time with God. I knew that I would be okay if I could just get to the beach and let God's love wash over me like the waves wash over the sand. So I drove to the beach and read, prayed, journaled, walked, listened—until peace came.

Dr. Richard Swensen says, "Our relationships are being starved to death by velocity" (as quoted in *Quiet Places* by Jane Rubietta). Try taking a walk and simply thank God for everything you see and appreciate in his creation. Or have your quiet time laying on your back in a field of daisies or a mountain meadow. Read Isaiah 40 or Genesis 1 from a mountain peak or ocean shore. Try taking photos of landscapes, sunsets, flowers or oceans. Then find verses that you think capture the essence of the photo. These can be framed, scanned into a computer for a screensaver or turned into a poster, postcards or stationary.

Nature can become a part of your daily quiet time. Create a backyard oasis where you can retreat to pray or read. Try a gazebo, a secret garden, a sunroom, patio, hammock or front porch swing and turn it into a meeting place between you and God.

10.

QUIET-TIME BASKETS

I love baskets. Small, large, wicker, twig, oval or heart-shaped—I love them all! Some of my baskets are simple, while others are lined with fabric or decorated with raffia or ribbon. I use my baskets as a quiet-time resource to enhance my times with God.

When I started putting together quiet-time baskets, I found myself spending more time with God. Having a quiet-time basket in nearly every room of my home (and a durable quiet-time box in the car) helps me to take time to connect to God no matter where my responsibilities take me.

In each basket I place a simple devotional like *Our Daily Bread,* a devotional-type Bible like IVP's *Quiet Time Bible,* or *The Message.* I usually tuck in a devotional classic like *My Upmost for His Highest, The Singer* or *Hinds Feet on High Places* and a devotional magazine like *Tapestry* or *Walk thru the Bible.* Many colleges and ministries offer these kind of magazines for a very affordable price.

I find that by having devotional material in user-friendly places I can stop and grab a minute with God while putting away laundry or straightening up the living room. I added a quiet-time journal and pen and my study Bible to the one in my dining room because that is where I most often have my quiet times. I even tucked some devotional material at the landing at the top of the stairs. When I see these baskets sprinkled throughout my home, I am reminded to use them!

I use bags for this same purpose. When life gets fast-paced, I have two or three canvas bags that hold inspirational reading, letters from important ministries and magazines. I carry these as I travel, when I go to sports practice—or anywhere I think I might end up waiting. I even carry a portion of the Bible in loose-leaf form in my organizer. This way when I am waiting during a few minutes at a carpool stop, I can meet God.

Men might find that those little Gideon Bibles tucked in book bags, workout bags and glove compartments serve well to remind them to stop and meet God. I've seen devotional material carried in toolboxes, tackle boxes and briefcases.

The key to quiet times on the run is to plan ahead.

The Bible encourages me to hide God's Word in my heart—but I've found I'm better at this if I first hide God's Word in every nook and cranny of my life.

11.

A SONG IN MY HEART

Teresa was coming home from a hospital visit to her mother. She was concerned about her mom. Her heart was heavy, and she was talking to God about her feelings. As she prayed, a melody came clearly into her mind. She then began weaving her feelings and the melody together into a song.

> You are the Rock of my salvation.
> You are the strength of my life.
> You are my hope and my inspiration.
> Lord, unto you do I cry.
>
> I believe in you, believe in you,

and your faithful love to me.
You have been my help in time of need.
Lord, unto you do I cleave.

("You Are the Rock of My Salvation" by Teresa Muller)

I have many friends who are songwriters, and the more I know of them and their lives, the more I see that they have cultivated the skill of worship. Each of them has decided to sing when they are sad and sing when they are happy.

Sing to God

For me it is so comforting to sing my way through my well-worn old red hymnal. The lyrics are so deep and rich. As I sing, the familiar sights and sounds of my childhood and youth flood back over me and I feel safe. I am also comforted by the thought that believers throughout the centuries and around the world have sung some of those same words.

In the same way, singing praise choruses is comforting because so often the words come straight from the Bible, often even word for word. Because choruses are so easy to remember, learning them provides the added benefit of helping me memorize Scripture.

I think it is unfortunate that music has caused so much controversy in the church. Just as David's harp playing soothed Saul, music is a powerful tool to soothe inspire, convict hearts today. Try one of these musical quiet time ideas.

☐ Pull the lyric jacket out of a CD or cassette that you don't normally listen to. See if you can figure out what might have been going through the lyricist's mind or going on in his or her life when it was written.

☐ Buy a hymnal or see if your church has an old one sitting around and collecting dust that you can have. Try to sing as many hymns you know. Then try to figure out which are your favorites, which you'd like to be sung at your wedding, your baptism, your funeral or other significant events in your life. Make a list and place it in your Bible, safe-deposit box or life insurance papers.

☐ Many hymns are also based on Scripture text. I find it a challenge to link a song back to a verse or passage that might have been its inspiration. I am comforted as I recall the context, the stories that made the writers pen those words.

☐ Sing a praise chorus until you have it memorized—especially one that is straight from Scripture. Since I'm not very musically inclined, I like to sing along with CDs like "Integrity Praise."

☐ Try to put your favorite verse to a familiar tune. This is how some of our favorite hymns were created. Often deep spiritual words were set to barroom tunes because the people know how they went. I learned Philippians 4:8 by singing it to the tune of "These Are a Few of My Favorite Things" from *The Sound of Music.*

☐ Put on a purely instrumental recording. Have a cup of coffee or tea, take a walk (with Walkman) or cook up a treat while you meditate on God's goodness in your life.

☐ Try writing a poem or story that could be set to music. Maybe there is a turning point in your faith you'd like to highlight or a change of heart God wrought in your life. Mix the mediums of art, photography, cinematography and music to create a memorable moment of inspiration.

❑ Read a book, such as *A Hymn Is Born* by Clint Bonner, that describes the story behind a hymn.

These quiet times will help you to make music a place of refuge in the Lord.

12.

FROM GOD'S HEART TO YOURS

I was very positive about moving to San Diego. I believed that exciting new opportunities were ahead for both Bill and me.

Bill was twenty-eight and a senior pastor. We moved from a booming megachurch to a small, recovering church. We left a three-bedroom, two-bathroom house that we'd totally remodeled and moved into a postage-stamp-sized apartment. Depression blindsided me.

As I went to the closet one day to get something, I reached up for boxes and they tumbled down. I couldn't even remember what I'd gone in there to get. I sat down on top of a dirty load of laundry and began to cry. My oldest son, age four, came toddling in and said, "Mommy, what's wrong?"

I very profoundly whined, "I don't know!"

Then I sat on top of that dirty load of laundry and rocked back and forth until the boys fell asleep in my arms. I put Zach in his crib and laid Brock in his bed and went and sat at the kitchen table.

Then I did what any red-blooded girl would do, I got on the phone and called a girlfriend. I whined and complained for over an hour, long distance. Then as only a best friend can do, Mary said, "Pam, what character trait, what attribute of God are you forgetting?"

I said, "Well, pretty much all of them!"

I hung up the phone and went back to the kitchen table. I took out my Bible; I skimmed through, writing down verses that had been underlined, starred or asterisked. Then I simply reworded those verses in a way that emphasized the attributes of God that spoke to my situation.

Nothing is impossible for Me. I am able to do immeasurably more than all you can ask or think. In Me all things were created, in heaven and on earth, visible and invisible, . . . thrones . . . powers . . . rulers . . . authorities. All things were created by Me and I am before all things and in Me all things hold together.

Mine is the greatness and the power and the glory and the majesty and the splendor . . . I am exalted as head over all. Wealth and honor come from Me. In My hands are strength and power to exalt . . . Nothing on earth is My equal!

It is not by your might nor by your power but by My

Spirit . . . I know when you sit down and when you rise; I perceive your thoughts from afar . . . I am familiar with all your ways. Before a word is on your tongue I know it completely . . . You cannot flee from My presence. If you go up to the heavens, I am there; If you make your bed in the depths, I am there. If you rise on the wings of the dawn, if you settle on the far side of the sea, even there My hand will guide you, My right hand will hold you fast . . . even the darkness is as light to Me.

I stretch out the heavens like a canopy and spread them out like a tent to dwell in . . . I measure the waters of the earth in the hallow of My hand, and with the breadth of My hand I mark off the heavens.

I am the Creator. I am the Wonderful Counselor, the Mighty God, the Everlasting Father, the Prince of Peace. I am the Alpha and Omega, . . . the beginning and the end.

I am immortal and dwell in unapproachable light . . . [Yet I tell you] approach My throne of grace with confidence, so that you may receive mercy and find grace to help in time of need.

I do not grow tired or weary, I have understanding no one can fathom . . . My judgments are unsearchable, My paths . . . beyond tracing out! My thoughts are precious and vast are the sum of them! No one fully understands My mind . . . No one instructed Me. No one taught Me the right way . . . No one can compare. . . .

I hem you in before and behind . . . be convinced that neither death nor life, neither angels nor demons, neither present nor the future nor any powers, neither height not depth nor anything else in all creation can separate you from My love that is in Christ Jesus your Lord. (Paraphrased from Matthew 17:20; Ephesians 3:20; Colossians 1:16-17; 1 Chronicles 29:11-12; Job 41:33;

Zechariah 4:6; Psalm 139:1-2; Isaiah 40; Isaiah 9:6; Revelation 22:13; 1 Timothy 6:16; Hebrews 4:16; Romans 11:33; Romans 8:38-40.)

I needed a fresh view of God and personalizing the Word tore the cataract off my heart and gave me a glimpse of the Creator. I needed to move what I knew of the Bible from my head to my heart. There can be power in spending a quiet time personalizing Scripture.

From My Heart to Yours

Writing out a paraphrase of favorite passages can also make a great quiet time if you are feeling like you are carrying a burden for another person. Finding verses that comfort someone else draws us into God's presence and we ourselves are comforted. For example, a friend of mine had a terminally ill friend whom she wanted to give a special gift of encouragement to, so she compiled verses about how personal God is and how available God can be.

Verses can be located by using an exhaustive concordance or computer Bible program. Simply brainstorm key words that might lead you to verses that would help. You might need to take the key words and find biblical words that are similar. For example, stress is a very common feeling, but the word *stress* isn't in the Bible. The words *perseverance, endure, endurance, long-suffering* are. Sometimes it's helpful to look for opposites. For example, if you are struggling with worry, look up *peace*.

What struggles are hitting your life or the lives of the ones you love? Brainstorm a list of words you can look up to find verses of comfort and hope.

13.

LOUD TIMES

Quiet times really don't have to be quiet. After all, faith does come by hearing (Romans 10:17).

While we served in youth ministry, each January our senior pastor called an all-church week-long Sabbath. All activities were canceled. The only thing that took place that week was the twenty-four hour a day reading aloud of God's Word. A part of the tradition of that event was that people would read for an hour and then stay and listen for an hour. I thought the time would drag; and I was sure we'd end up reading those passages in Leviticus. Was I surprised how quickly the time flew and how much I enjoyed reading and listening to the Word! (Even though we really did get some seemingly obscure passage.)

Try reading the Bible out loud even if you are by yourself. Or listen while your children read the Bible aloud. Or pick up a dramatized version of the Bible on audio or video.

On the Road
Having quiet times while on a family vacation can be a

challenge, but with some creativity it is possible. The key is that quiet times in the car need to be *loud*. Here are some ways we have done it.

☐ On long road trips, Bill and I start in Genesis and recite aloud every verse or piece of a verse we know from memory, continuing book-by-book through the entire Bible. As our kids have gotten older, they have joined in the game too.

☐ On the radio locate the talk show that you most disagree with and formulate arguments. Bonus points are given to the family member who can back their argument with Scripture.

☐ Listen to audio tapes of *Adventure in Odyssey*. Yes I know, it is a children's radio program, but our family thinks it is better than those *Mystery Theater* and *Green Hornet* radio dramas that Bill and I were reared on. There is always a biblical message, so it works well for a family quiet time on the go.

☐ Bill Bright says if he is with someone for more than five minutes, he considers it a divine appointment, so he shares his faith. Challenge your family to share Jesus all along the way. Provide them with tracts, ideas and practical ways to move conversations from the mundane to the spiritual.

Have your quiet time out loud—chances are someone who is listening may need to hear it.

14.

ACT ONE—
SCENE ONE

My soul glorifies in the Lord,
   and my spirit rejoices in God my Savior,
for he has been mindful
   of the humble state of his servant.
From now on all generations will call me blessed,
   for the Mighty One has done great things for me—
   holy is his name. (Luke 1:46-49)

One of my favorite quiet times was when I memorized
Mary's response to the angel telling her she was to bear the
Messiah. As I sought to capture her heart at such at magnifi-
cent moment, I was brought to tears. The more I read the
words aloud, the more they meant to me. I researched that
section of Scripture to gain a deeper meaning through
commentaries and word study helps. Then I read it aloud
again, seeking to memorize it. I was so moved, I shared it
with my husband and children—then I shared it in front of

the church during the Christmas season!

The Bible will come alive if you memorize it and act it out. I have seen whole books of the Bible reenacted—word for word. It is a moving experience. Try memorizing some of the outstanding prayers of the Bible like Hannah's outpouring for a child (1 Samuel 2), the dedication of the temple (2 Chronicles 6) or the Lord's Prayer (Matthew 6:9-13).

When I was a child, I learned the Lord's Prayer in Indian sign language from my next-door neighbor, a devout believer from the reservation. Now, over thirty years later, I can still sign that song for the Lord in prayer.

Get your family involved. Reenact the Christmas story or the parting of the Red Sea using the exact words of the text. One person can narrate while the others play a part. Max Lucado brags about his wife's creativity when their family reenacted the manna falling from heaven by placing the bread on the ceiling fan blades—then flipping the switch!

If you are stage shy, then try listening to the dramatized version of the Bible or the new Bible on video. Or for a real change of pace, listen to the radio when dramatized sections of Scripture are a part of the listening schedule—often around Easter or Christmas. Or try your hand at writing a script with a storyline that includes pieces of Scripture. The station manager of the largest talk-radio station in San Diego, KOGO, wrote and was part of an on-air performance reenacting the Christmas story from a journalist's point of view—now that is a fresh viewpoint!

Memorization accompanied with action etches the Word of God into your heart. Lights, camera, action!

15.

Chart Your
Course

Write a letter to God about your life. What would you like to see happen in the next three to six months? What would you like to learn about God? How would you like to change or grow? What requests would you like answered? Maybe you are at a special juncture in life, have an obstacle to hurdle or a circumstance you'd like to see change. Write out your feelings, goals and requests.

Place your letter in a self-addressed stamped envelope. Give the letter to a friend to mail back to you after three, six or twelve months. Or place it in a prominent place, like your Bible, with a date written on the outside, then open it on that date.

I found this idea helpful after the death of my father. I took a limited sabbatical from responsibilities as director of women for a few months following my father's death because I was executor of his will. But after two months I still wasn't feeling emotionally better. I wrote a letter to God about how I wanted to feel at the one-year anniversary of my father's death. As I wrote the letter, I realized I was not going to be able to make this journey alone. I wrote down books to read. I contacted a grief counselor. I wrote out activities that I thought would help me resolve my feelings and bring closure to the loss of my dad. Now, ten months into the journey, I believe I am much further along in my grief than I would have been if I had not taken this quiet time with God to verbalize how I need him to heal me.

Some people use this to aid in healing after loss of a job, a marriage or a child. There are some journeys we don't want to go on, but writing to God about the difficult path ahead makes the road less formidable.

Pull out the stationary and write away.

16.

QUESTIONS OF
THE HEART

What would you like to ask God when you get to heaven?
Spend a quiet time writing out a list of theological
questions that you'd love to know the answer to. Which
doctrines do you need to learn more about: eschatology
(end times), the person of Christ, the Holy Spirit, baptism, sin or sanctification? List those. Pick out some heavy
doctrinal words you'd like to know the meaning of such
as *theophany, eschatology, dispensationalism, Calvinism, cove-
nant* or *propitiation*.

After you've written a list of questions, go to a Christian bookstore and buy a book that will help you study
and learn the answers. You might try asking your pastor
what theology books he or she had to read in seminary
or Bible college. You may want to pick up a concordance,
a Bible dictionary, an encyclopedia, a church-history
book or an atlas.

One of my favorite quiet times was tracing how the

Bible came from its original language written on papyrus to the English version that I enjoy. That study led me deep into church history into the lives of Tyndale, Wycliffe and others who risked their lives to bring the Bible to people in their own language. What started out to be a one-day quiet time turned into a several month journey that enriched my view of how precious the Bible is.

Seeker Questions

Think of questions people who don't know Jesus ask. Make a list and research biblical responses. Keep these quiet times, file them or use a computer publisher program to add graphics so they'll be ready to give away.

For me these quiet times have later come in very handy in talking with others. For example, I have answers to questions like: Why should I wait until marriage for sex? Why should I believe the Bible? What makes Jesus so special? What happens to people who don't accept Jesus? What is heaven like? What is hell like? What does God have to say that will help me be a better parent? Why should my family go to church on Easter? How do I know that God created the earth and when did he do it?

Keep Asking

One of my favorite quiet times was a set of interviews in which I asked people who had walked with Jesus for thirty to fifty years, "Why do you still believe, and what has held your faith together all these years?" It was interesting to listen for commonalties. The main one was God's faithfulness to them *amidst their questioning*.

He's waiting—what do you want to ask?

17.

PRECIOUS PROMISES

Julie is a beautiful young mother with a gorgeous daughter, Sarah. Most people seeing Sarah would not know she is very ill and has been her entire life. Julie, for over seven years, has collected verses that comfort her and verses that proclaim God's ability to be Sarah's strength and hope. When Sarah is in the hospital, those verses, written on 3 x 5 cards, are a constant companion.

Recently, when Sarah had surgery, Julie created 3 x 5 cards for friends and church family. Each card had one of those favorite verses and a picture of Sarah. We were to pray for Sarah, using that verse as a springboard to our prayers. As Julie was having her hospital-bedside quiet times, she knew we were all having quiet times that included Sarah too. That verse and Sarah's picture were posted on my PC and my refrigerator so I would be reminded to pray. It also reminds me of the power of passing on a promise. As we give away our personal devotional life, God gives back.

One of the churches that hosted me as a speaker passed on a perpetual calendar filled with verses that had been personalized with my name inserted. A small group committed to use a calendar with my name in it to pray for me each day. What a gift!

Families can stay connected by reading God's promises together. One Christmas my mother gave every daughter and daughter-in-law in the family the same quiet time book and journal. When we saw each other throughout the year, we shared promises that we had gleaned from God for our own lives—and each other's.

You might decide to create 3 x 5 cards, a small journal or a perpetual calendar. To make a calendar, simply have 365 index cards or similar-sized paper bound together at your local printer. Creating your own Bible promise book can help you navigate the pain of grief, divorce, illness or job loss. God knows what your pain is and his Word can be a healing balm.

Today, try to think of a creative way to pass on a promise. In the process you'll probably notice that some of God's promises have become very precious to you.

18.

Versions

Sometimes when we read and reread passages, they become such familiar territory that we don't see the Word afresh. But God's Word is alive! We need to find ways to hear the words of Scripture as if we were reading them for the first time.

One way to do this is to read a different translation or to read a variety of translations to gain a different perspective on the same passage. You can also buy a parallel Bible that contains several translations so that as you have a quiet time, you can read across the versions to gain insights. For example, look at Matthew 11:28-30 in the following Bible versions.

Come unto me, all ye that labour and are heavy laden, and I will give you rest. Take my yoke upon you, and learn of me; for I am meek and lowly in heart: and ye shall find rest unto your souls. For my yoke is easy, and my burden is light. (King James Version)

Come to me, all you who are weary and burdened, and I

will give you rest. Take my yoke upon you and learn from me, for I am gentle and humble in heart, and you will find rest for your souls. For my yoke is easy and my burden is light. (New International Version)

Come to Me, all you who labor and are heavy–laden and overburdened, and I will cause you to rest. (I will ease and relieve and refresh your souls.) Take my yoke upon you and learn from Me, for I am gentle (meek) and humble (lowly) in heart, and you will find rest (relief and ease and refreshment and recreation and blessed quiet) for your souls. For My yoke is wholesome (useful, good— not harsh, hard, sharp, or pressuring, but comfortable, gracious, and pleasurable), and My burden is light and easy to be borne. (Amplified)

Are you tired? Worn out? Burned out on religion? Come to Me. Get away with me and you'll recover your life. I'll show you how to take real rest. Walk with me and work with me—watch how I do it. Learn the unforced rhythms of grace. I won't lay anything heavy or ill-fitting on you. Keep company with me and you'll learn to live freely and lightly. (The Message)

Come to me and I will give you rest—all you who work so hard beneath a heavy yoke. Wear my yoke—for it fits perfectly—and let me teach you; for I am gentle and humble, and you shall find rest for your souls; for I give light burdens. (The Living Bible)

Come to me, all of you who are tired and have heavy loads. I will give you rest. Accept my work and learn from me I am gentle and humble in spirit. And you will find rest for your souls. The work that I ask you to carry is not heavy. (The International Children's Version)

If you've been reading the same Bible for years, try out another version—so you can look at the Word through fresh eyes.

19.

HOLD FAST

Fasting is almost a lost discipline. Either people treat it as a legalistic, strong-arm technique to get God to grant their petition, or it is connected only to health issues like purifying one's body. The most encouraging benefit of fasting is sometimes overlooked because it is so simple: fasting changes our pace, our focus and our hearts so we have fewer distractions. A fast gives us quality time with God.

My favorite experience with fasting came when Bill and I were looking to move from youth ministry to the senior pastorate. Because it was such a big move and we really had no idea where we thought God wanted us to locate geographically, we set aside a day to pray and fast.

All day I asked God to simply help me ask the right questions, help me know what kind of a decision-making grid he wanted us to use. As I would think of one, I'd jot it down. By the end of the day I had a list of nearly twenty things we should be looking for in the next ministry location.

When Bill got home, he had his own list, and when we compared them, they were nearly identical! This helped greatly in candidating because when opportunities came, we used this grid God impressed upon us as the standard by which we made our choice.

Fasting is almost an "of course" in the Old Testament. The nation of Israel treated it as a part of prayer, meditation and mourning. It was a normal part of their lives. As the examples which follow show, fasting is woven through both the Old and New Testaments.

Times of Mourning

" Then John's disciples came and asked him, 'How is it that we and the Pharisees fast, but your disciples do not fast?'

"Jesus answered, 'How can the guests of the bridegroom mourn while he is with them? The time will come when the bridegroom will be taken from them; then they will fast'" (Matthew 9:14-15).

Times of Decision-Making

"They proclaimed a fast and seated Naboth in a prominent place among the people" (1 Kings 21:12).

For Consecration to God

"Alarmed, Jehoshaphat resolved to inquire of the LORD,

and he proclaimed a fast for all Judah" (2 Chronicles 20:3).

For Repentance
"The Ninevites believed God. They declared a fast, and all of them, from the greatest to the least, put on sackcloth" (Jonah 3:5).

For God's Favor
"Go, gather together all the Jews who are in Susa, and fast for me. Do not eat or drink for three days, night or day. I and my maids will fast as you do. When this is done, I will go to the king, even though it is against the law. And if I perish, I perish" (Esther 4:16)

With Wrong Motives
Your fasting ends in quarreling and strife,
    and in striking each other with wicked fists.
You cannot fast as you do today
    and expect your voice to be heard on high.
Is this the kind of fast I have chosen,
    only a day for a man to humble himself?
Is it only for bowing one's head like a reed
    and for lying on sackcloth and ashes?
Is that what you call a fast,
    a day acceptable to the Lord? (Isaiah 58:4-5)

"I fast twice a week and give a tenth of all I get" (the Rich Young Ruler in Luke 18:12).

To Overcome Sin
"To loose the bonds of wickedness, to set the oppressed

free, and break every yoke" (Isaiah 58:6).

"This kind [of demon] does not go out except by prayer
and fasting" (Matthew 17:21).

How to Fast

There are three basic types of fasting from food options.
The *absolute* fast means nothing to eat or drink. This one
is possible for one meal, but a regular intake of water is
necessary for life. The *partial* fast limits food and drink
to juices and water and sometimes herb teas and soups
and vegetable broths. The *normal* fast is no food and only
water to drink. In the Bible there are examples of one-,
three-, seven- and forty-day fasts. The longer you decide
to fast, the more you should read about fasting first.
Consulting your physician is wise as well.

Your personality and life situation may affect how you
fast. I have seen the recipe for the juice mixture that Bill
Bright, the president of Campus Crusade for Christ, uses
for a forty-day fast. It may have been great for Bill, but for
me it was so complex that I would have been distracted
by all the preparations. It would have defeated the whole
reason I usually fast—to gain more quiet time with God
to listen. Mothers or those married to unbelievers may
need to have shorter fasts or may be interrupted by
responsibilities. Remember, it isn't more "spiritual" to fast
a certain way. You are simply trying to strengthen your
connection to God.

Fasting should be accompanied by rest. Fasting can
affect your physical strength, so light exercise and lots of
water are wise components also. When coming off a

prolonged fast of more that a meal or two, you should be careful to eat bland foods in small amounts first.

It isn't just food that can rob our time and our hearts from God. Other ways to fast are to skip your favorite TV program and have a quiet time instead or to take a mental-health day from housework or your normal work routine. Or cut out the chocolate, cola or coffee that seem to have a habitual hold on you. You might fast from listening to your talk-radio or rock station in the car as you drive and pray instead.

Anytime you break the routine and give God the time, he is faithful to meet you there. Give up something to gain more.

20.

JUST DO IT!

We're a T-shirt society. Give us a slogan, cause or catchy saying, and we'll wear it on our back.

I listen to sermons frequently. I write them. I preach them. Yet only a few stick out in my mind. One was a series Jill Briscoe did for leaders. Every day in every message Jill would use the Nike commercial slogan and say, *Just Do It!* Then she'd teach a principle for leadership and all though it would be the saying: *Just Do It!* One day it was *Do It Tired.* Next, *Do It Scared.* Then, *Do It Bad Until You Can Do It Good.*

Now in ministry when I am so exhausted I can't think or feel I can't go on, I hear a gentle reminder, *Just do it. Do it tired!* On those days I don't feel like having my quiet time I hear *Just do it!*

I like to take what I am learning in my Bible studies and devotional times and capture its essence in a phrase. I designed a T-shirt to go with a talk I give on perseverance. On the front it has a cross. On the back: *He went the distance for me, I can live this moment for him!*

I know that perseverance is a complex subject. There are hundreds of verses on the topic, but when I am dead tired what keeps me motivated is that saying, that word picture in my mind of all Jesus did on the cross for me. When I'm tired I can't process a long spiritual treatise, but I can remember to take one more step for him.

Try it! See if you can create an internal motivating saying for one of these spiritual disciplines: prayer, fasting, worship, Bible study or holiness. Think of how it might fit on a coffee mug, T-shirt or commercial.

Some might think this is making the holy into something trite, but *obedience is never trite.* If it helps you remember to obey his Word, *Just Do It!*

21.

MIRACLE SCRAPBOOK

The first year we were married I knew we were headed for a life in ministry. I began a scrapbook that would capture in picture form the answers to prayer that it took to get us into full-time ministry. Someday we'd have children, and I didn't want them to think because we were in ministry we were paid to be good. (I wanted them to know there was a time when we were "good for nothing!")

I began to keep evidence of answered prayer. For example, the grocery bags that held two weeks worth of free groceries we received when we were broke and not really sure how many days we could stretch five dollars. I gathered receipts, notecards, photos and our prayer journal sheets to show how God worked when we moved from one apartment to another.

During this same time our car died (a green Vega with a blue back door—no great loss except that it was our only car!) We rode our bikes everywhere Bill's senior year of college. I was already working full-time and Bill was working part-time, so we really did need God to step in provide the car. We prayed. Our youth group prayed. The first page of the miracle scrapbook has a bumper sticker one of the kids gave us for our car-to-be that said "I believe in miracles!" and nine months and many pages into the scrapbook—our car arrived. I have a picture of us and the green Chevy Impala that we bought for the cost of a brake job. Most of the high-school students that were a part of that youth group are now serving in ministry, and I can't help to think that praying for that Impala had something to do with it.

Whenever my faith becomes weary and I'm not sure if God can see me, our church, our family or our para-church ministry through a crisis or challenge, I pull out that miracle scrapbook. I am reminded that while the obstacles might have changed or grown, God hasn't changed, and he is able to handle the challenge.

My children love that book too because they get a glimpse of our hearts before they were born. And now with our oldest approaching young adulthood, he fully appreciates the faith in God that was built during those early years together.

Putting It Together

There are many ways to go back and compile a scrapbook. You can interview people who were a part of some of your steps of faith. You can gather photographs. You can recreate a spiritual adventure with the help of postcards, magazines and brochures. You can also put the graphics of your computer to work and create separate pages of steps of faith you took: we believed God for school, we believed God for each other, we believed God for children, we believed God for a home, and we believed God for a career. Use different color pages and write in your memories.

In the movie *Twister* the two lead characters being chased by a tornado take leather straps and strap themselves together then strap themselves to a pipe that goes thirty feet in the ground. The twister turns them upside down into the eye of the storm, but they come out unscathed—why? They strapped themselves to an immovable object strong enough to withstand the wind.

Ecclesiastes 4:9-12 says, "Two are better than one . . . a cord of three strands is not quickly broken." By recording anchor points in your marriage or family, you strengthen the faith of everyone in that family. By spending your quiet times cataloging God's provision for you, your heartstring to him is also strengthened.

22.

SILENCE

"Be still and know that I am God."

Pagers. Fax machines. Cell phones. Headphones. There is no white space anymore. You know, the margin around the printed page of a book, the empty space around a letter, the quiet place without TV background noise or radio static. Enjoying quiet is a lost art.

For me, meeting God as a child meant a walk to the back pasture and sitting on a woodplank and dangling my toes into the cool ditchwater. I'd walk to the apple orchard and pack a picnic lunch for one. I'd sit and gaze over the horizon about sunset perched from a rock or the top of the lambing shed or haystack. I often went on these adventures late Sunday afternoon, while everyone else in my home watched football. I looked at creation and talked to the Creator. Now, with years of ministry under my belt, I still think those times of solitude were some of my best times with God. I think it was because *I listened*.

Many of us miss God in the everyday, but when things

are still, when we take time in the quietness of nature—or the quietness of our souls—our hearts will begin to tune into thoughts of God. In quietness the deeper questions of life arise: *Why am I here? Who created all of this? What will happen when this earthly body no longer houses my soul? What is the purpose of life?*

Sometimes God seems to be silent, but the problem may actually be that we aren't listening. In Romans 1:20 Paul explains that even in nature, we are led to God: "For since the creation of the world God's invisible qualities—his eternal power and divine nature—have been clearly seen, being understood from what has been made, so that men are without excuse."

Finding Places

After I went to college, I was afraid I'd lose my opportunities for solitude. But I found the college campus was very empty on Sunday afternoons, so I could still pack a picnic for one.

Then I married and moved into an apartment. Where would I find any solitude here? The park, schoolyards, downtown city benches. I just tried to seek my solitude by swimming upstream going where people wouldn't be that time of day or that day of the week.

Now I make it a point to log places of solitude in my mind as I spot them from the freeway or see them on errands. Being a woman, I look for places that I can be alone but safe.

Annie Dillard quotes the prophet Ezekiel who chastises false prophets who have "not gone up into the gaps." Dillard says: "The gaps are the thing. The gaps are the spirit's home, the altitude and latitudes so dazzlingly spare and clean that the spirit can discover itself for the first time like a once blind man unbound . . . . Stalk the gaps. Squeak into a gap . . . . This is how you spend this afternoon, and tomorrow morning, and tomorrow afternoon. *Spend the afternoon.* You can't take it with you."

When was the last time you went into the gap—into nature—and looked for the evidences of God's fingerprints?

Begin with the Roses

Find a garden. If it's been awhile since you stopped to smell the roses, do just that. Begin your journey in solitude by a walk in a garden or park. Find a grassy knoll and lay on your back and count the stars or if by day, watch the clouds, noting their shapes. Then just pray through your thoughts as they come, even if they seem jumbled and random.

Thank God. Try complimenting God on things you see around you. I have always loved turning over the dirt and finding those cute rolly-polly bugs. They remind me how marvelously creative God is!

Play hooky with Jesus. Set aside a morning to sleep in, read books about who God is like *Knowledge of the Holy, Knowing God, The Jesus I Never Knew.* Rent some of the Christian videos classics like *The Robe, Ten Commandments* or *Ben Hur.* Or lay by a pool and read a novel that will help you appreciate God, like Francine Rivers' *Redeeming Love* or her Mark of the Lion series.

It may feel strange at first to rest in the Lord, but one day of R and R with God can give you back months of clarity and productivity.

23.

HIGH-TECH CONNECTIONS

Fax, e-mail, voicemail, Internet, personal recording de-vices—there are so many ways to stay connected in to-day's high-tech world. But can any of these be used to impact our connection with God?

Sound Ideas

Personally, I love my walkman. I pop in a Bible-study tape or a praise-music tape and I can connect with God while on a walk in a noisy city, crowded airport or cramped plane seat. I recently found myself on a packed flight surrounded by people determined not to connect inter-personally. I was tired when I turned on the headset, but my soul was renewed because a brand new Christmas album of Christian tunes was on the airline radio menu! Life suddenly looked a whole lot brighter as I looked out of the window at the twinkling city lights and was re-minded of God's individual love and care for all who dwelled below.

You might try recording encouraging verses into a personal key ring recorder and playing them back throughout the day or reading a favorite verse into a friend's voicemail. Then they can return the favor.

Log On

If you get to work or start on that day-long term paper assignment and realize you haven't had your quiet time, use a break time to log onto the net and surf a devotional page like the ones that follow.

☐ www.christiannet.demon.co.uk

☐ www.electriciti.com/pkennedy/devotional.htm

☐ www.gospelcom.net/devotionals (This one has an entire page of all kinds of devotional material from some of Christianity's most reliable ministries.)

These are just a few. In about five minutes I found over fifty devotional options on the net.

Design It

Put your own expertise to work by designing a computer game or screensaver that builds your devotional life. Use a personal recording device to record prayers, devotional thoughts or memory verses that you can review throughout the day. Or scan in your favorite photo, choose a favorite verse, then print it out and you have a poster! We captured each one of our three boys in action at their favorite sport, had them chose a verse to go with the picture and then had the whole thing blown up to 18 x 20. They each have an inspirational poster of themselves in living color on their walls.

In Deuteronomy 11:18-21 God encourages the reader: "Fix these words of mine in your hearts and minds; tie them as symbols on your hands and bind them on your foreheads. . . . Write them on the doorframes of your houses and on your gates." I think personal computers are today's equivalent to writing on the doorframes and gates—after all, many of us open up "windows" on our computers every day. Make some of those windows an encouragement from God's Word.

24.

THE BIG SPLURGE

Sometimes I feel like splurging on my relationship with God. I escape to a friend's garden. Or I bring out the best china and have hand-dipped chocolates or fresh homemade scones with specialty teas as I sit and take in precious gems from God's Word. Or we curl up together, I in a windowseat cushioned with pillows, and God enthroned on high.

Since my relationship with God is vital to all the rest of my life, I don't like to shortchange my time with him. I regularly look for an extra day to spend in solitude at a cozy mountain cabin. I grab a few moments of prayer in an art gallery. I devour devotional books as I recline poolside. I've always been on a budget—yet have always looked for ways to make my time with God special, out of the ordinary.

At times I want my relationship with God to be white linen, crystal, rose petals and lace. I buy journals with blank pages inside and works of art on the outside. I want to look forward to my time with God in much the same way as I look forward to a week in Hawaii with my husband. I want some of my quiet times to remind me of how I felt as a little girl in my new white patent-leather Mary Janes and bonnet on Easter Sunday.

Make It Special

Splurge on your relationship with God. Try these unique quiet times.

☐ *The victory*. Go to a place that signifies winning to you: the ballpark, the end zone, the winner's circle. Take a set of verses on victory through God and reflect on how God has turned you into a champion.

☐ *The Eden experience*. Find a garden and take along your favorite journal, drawing pad, paints or handiwork. Sit quietly and take in just a tiny glimpse of what could have been before Eve ate the apple. Try to express back to God your thanks that even though sin entered the world in the Garden, God redeemed humankind. God is the

Creator, and since you are made in his image, try some creativity in his presence. Try poetry, photography or painting. Don't worry how good it is. You are his kid. Parents love to display their children's art work on the refrigerator—no matter what the quality—because their child created it.

The five star. Spend a contemplative weekend in a resort or other five-star accommodation. Or turn your own home into a bed-and-breakfast. Pull out the china, crystal and lace pillows and have a tea party with God. Or enjoy breakfast in bed while you have your devotions. Read all the verses about rest, sabbath and repose. For example, Isaiah 28:12-13 says: " 'This is the resting place, let the weary rest'; and 'This is the place of repose'—but they would not listen. So then, the word of the LORD to them will become: Do and do, do and do, rule on rule, rule on rule."

Mountain-top experience. Go to the highest spot in your city and pray there. Picnic on a hill or a rooftop and catch a sunrise or sunset. Spend time on the top of a professional building—anyplace where you get a better view. This is a terrific time to spend time with God reprioritizing because things that seem huge look smaller from on high.

I know these can't be everyday quiet-time experiences, but I find that if I have a few of these sprinkled throughout my year, I keep a better perspective on life as a whole. Maybe it is because these are special events that slow my pace and my thoughts. I regain clarity and composure as I draw into God's presence for a longer period of time.

25.

ANOTHER POINT OF VIEW

Lon and Leah Knievel are working in the Iteri tribe in Papua New Guinea. When translating the Parable of the Sower, they were looking for the best word for good soil. Their language guide took them to a place and showed them deep, rich soil that had formed through the decay of the best trees. It was "mulchy" soil. In that tribe having a heart before God that is good and ready to grow most closely resembles a compost pile!

Hearing these new ways of translating God's Word has inspired and enriched my quiet times because understanding the process gives more depth to words and phrases. For example, when I learn American Sign Language for biblical words, those words become richer and more alive as I come across them in a quiet time.

Make friends with a missionary, writing to him or her may enrich your quiet times, as will a friendship with someone of a different language group.

Discover God in Another Culture

I have also had my heart renewed as I have visited churches from other cultures. I have been inspired by my friend Mesghina Gebremedhin, a professor at Biola University who is working with international students in the Los Angeles area. Years ago he and his wife had to flee a murderous communist regime in their African region of Eritreia. Mesghina began a church for refugees of his native country who were fleeing to the "safety" of Los Angeles.

I had the opportunity to attend a worship service with him and his family. Even though I understood very few words, I was captivated by one of the songs. The chorus kept repeating, "Oh, Mesghina. Oh, Mesghina." After the service, I asked Mesghina why the church was singing about him.

Almost embarrassed, he looked down humbly and said, "Mesghina means 'praise the Lord' in my language."

Mesghina has one of the most sincere hearts of any man I have met. He simply loves Christ and is totally devoted to helping his people come to grips with God's goodness despite the painful past they have endured. God's gentle perseverance is now easier for me to picture because I watched people of another culture sing, "Oh, Mesghina!"

If you can't find a church of a different culture in your area, then you can be equally inspired by books. *From Jerusalem to Irian Jaya* or *The Global Prayer Digest* are both resources that will give you a glimpse of the lives of believers around the world. One of my favorite devotional experiences with my children was reading the book *From Arapesh to Zuni*, a Wycliffe resource that depicts tribes that still need a Bible in their own language. As we prayed for each tribe, God gave me a new appreciation for the privilege of owning a Bible that I can read at any time.

Meditate on these verses and ask God how and where you might step out of your comfort zone and into another's shoes:

He is the atoning sacrifice for our sins, and not only for ours but also for the sins of the whole world. (1 John 2:2)

After this I looked and there before me was a great multitude that no one could count, from every nation, tribe, people and language, standing before the throne and in front of the Lamb. They were wearing white robes and were holding palm branches in their hands. (Revelation 7:9)

26.

Gift to God

Each year at Christmas I like to take a quiet time and consider what gift I'd like to give to God in the next year. Sometimes it's a monetary donation to an organization that will help the Bible get integrated into people's lives. Sometimes it's a spiritual commitment that will help the Bible get better applied to my own heart.

Each person in our family writes out his or her gift to Jesus and places it in a white envelope on the Christmas tree. Those are the last and most precious gifts opened on Christmas morning.

When I speak at Christmas events, I share the idea of the white envelope and give attendees an opportunity to give a gift to Jesus. In the crowd at a gathering this past Christmas was a wonderful, young single woman, Kelly, who had come to the mountains with her mother to make a memory. Cancer had ravaged Kelly's body and her mother thought a quiet Christmas weekend in the mountains would be the best of medicine. Kelly agreed.

After everyone had departed, I gathered up the hundreds of white envelopes. I had committed to pray over each request, each gift, each person. When I got to Kelly's, it was I who received a gift. She wrote:

> With whatever time I have left on earth, by the grace of God, I will leave others with God's love. No matter what the cancer does to my body, no matter how bad I feel, I will share God's love with others.

Gift Ideas

☐ Send a gift to the person who led you to Christ or discipled you. One year I sent heart-shaped gifts to all the women who had encouraged my heart the year prior.

☐ Send a gift to the church(es) that have reached you and helped you grow. Or send a gift to a person who helped you grow. Try tracking down that second-grade Sunday-school teacher!

☐ Thank a school teacher. Prior to the Thanksgiving holiday one year, I called all of my son's public school teachers just to say thanks. It happened to be the same day report cards came home so I imagine my cheery voice was a welcome oasis to the numerous complaints that were on their voice mail. One of Brock's teachers returned the call just to say, "You made my day!"

☐ If you came to Christ as a teen or a young adult, try to picture what your life would have been like if you had come to Christ at a later date—then send a gift to a helping ministry like a crisis pregnancy clinic, a battered women's shelter, a rescue mission or a teen parachurch group.

☐ Send Bibles to places and people in need. Nearly every year someone in our family chooses to send Bibles somewhere around the world through the American Bible Society.

☐ Send a kid to camp. In one week at camp a child spends almost as much time learning about God as he or she would in six months of youth group. Often camp is the only way some kids hear about Jesus in a way they can accept him into their lives.

Christmas is a great time to celebrate the gift that was given to you by giving back.

27.

GOD IN THE EVERYDAY

One day I pulled a crystal glass out of my dishwasher and went to fill it with water. I had been exercising and was so dry. I filled it up to the brim with crystal clear drinking water from the refrigerator and lifted it to my lips. Just as I was about to take a big refreshing gulp, I spotted food particles crusted to the inside of the glass. I immediately tossed the water down the drain and reached for a clean glass.

I had been reading in my quiet time about the traits of a leader in the book of 2 Timothy, and I immediately remembered the passage: "If a man cleanses himself from the latter, he will be an instrument for noble purposes, made holy, useful to the Master and prepared to do any good work." (2 Timothy 2:21). I thought long and hard about that glass, and now, years later, when I sin and I want to keep the sin secret or justify it—I remember the glass and how I felt with it in my hand. I never want to be set aside like that glass.

Quiet times are a great time for object lessons. Howard Hendricks in his book *Living by the Book* points out that everyday items can be used as bridges of application. When Jesus taught in parable—consider this fig tree . . . a man was sowing seed . . . a woman lost a coin—he was using mundane objects to capture our imaginations and communicate great truths.

Pick up something from the coffee table or the desk. Look at an object in your kitchen. Take something out of your wallet or purse. Consider what Bible truth it might remind you of. Ask yourself, *What does this teach me about God?*

Try it! Your keys could help you ponder the keys to success in the Bible—the keys to healthy relationships, the key truths every Christian should know.

In the simple, God's wisdom can be profound. Ask God to use the everyday to connect you to his heart. Every day.

28

THE FIVE SENSES

I grew up on a sheep farm. In my home as a child, we had lamb pelts, and touching or smelling them reminded me of the good shepherd laying down his life for the sheep. I have a crown of thorns placed high on my favorite bookshelf as a reminder of the price Christ paid for me. Having visual reminders of Christ in prominent places helps me to carry that picture with me wherever I go.

We can use our five senses to make the sights, sounds, smells, taste and feel of the Bible real.

☐ Look through the Bible and note the smells, like Jesus being called the "Rose of Sharon."

☐ Gather up a few tasty treats from the Song of Solomon, then buy a recording of Hebrew music to listen to while you eat.

☐ Create a night to remember by renting a travel video of the Holy Land—or actually watch a slide show done by a friend who has been there. Make the whole evening the sights and sounds of Israel.

☐ Hang a nail from your Christmas-tree branches as a reminder of his death on the cross. Take time to meditate on the verses about Christ's death when you hang the nail.

I have a list going of things I'd love to have that would be similar reminders of Bible teaching. For example, an alabaster vial with perfume in it. The verses that describe the woman who broke her costly perfume—valued at over a year's salary—because of her deep appreciation of Christ's work in her life always moves me to tears. The verses that refer to our lives being a fragrant aroma and the songs of worship that remind me that Jesus was broken and his blood spilled out capture my heart. What captures yours?

Discover New Land

To grasp hold of the power of a "hands-on" experience of the Bible you might like to go an archeological dig or make a pilgrimage to the Holy Land or lower Europe where Paul took his many journeys. If being an armchair tourist better suits your taste, then pick up a novel that captures a period of church history, like Francine River's Mark of the Lion series, which walks the reader through life in a first-century setting.

You might try incorporating a traditional Jewish holiday into your own family traditions. Attend a Passover Seder or set up palm booths (a tent made of tree branches or palm fronds) in your yard and celebrate Purim and read the story of Esther. Many books are available at your local library and Christian bookstore that describe the Jewish calendar and festivals.

Picture This

You can use color to rev up your quiet-time experience. Use colored pencils to mark verses so you can find them more readily. An example would be to mark "the Roman Road" (Romans 1:16-17, 3:23, 6:23, 5:8, 10:9-10, 8:38-39) in your Bible so at any time you could have the information readily accessible to lead someone to Christ.

I like to mark my outlines and the main points of a passage with color. When studying the Proverbs 31 woman, I marked all the verbs in blue (and she was a woman of action): she does, she looks, she brings, she rises, she considers, she girds, she senses, she stretches, she extends, she is not afraid, she makes, she opens, she looks, and then her kids rise up and bless her. A set of colored pencils—or a twelve-colors-in-one pencil will color your quiet time.

Kay Arthur has encouraged more lively Bible study by instructing those in Precept studies to use simple drawings to help principles pop off the page. Use rainbows to mark promises, a sad face to mark sins to avoid, a happy face to mark the results of obedience. I mark my favorite chapters about Jesus being our shepherd with a little stick-figure lamb on the top corner of the page can help me found those chapters quickly when I need some encouragement in a hurry. There are many simple symbols—a heart, a light bulb, a question mark—that you can use to mark a text as you move through it. You don't have to be a Rembrandt; stick figures will do!

On occasion, make your quiet time more active, more colorful or accompany it with the sights and sounds of devotion. Be careful—this kind of hands-on-learning might become addictive because it's so much fun!

29.

SUPER SUNDAYS

Sunday can be a challenging day to have quiet times. Often in the rush of getting to church, we forget to meet with God! Here are some ways to use your quiet time to prepare to meet God at church and to continue praying and applying what you learn each week.

The Early Bird
Try going thirty minutes early to church. Sit quietly in the pew and pray that God will meet you and the others who come. Or as many pastors do, walk through the sanctuary and pray for each seat and the person that will be in that place to receive from God. You might also find a quiet spot on your church grounds to sit and read a psalm or sing a favorite hymn or chorus.

If possible, try walking to church. Or take a faith walk around the neighborhood where your church is located and pray for the neighborhood and the city.

Another quiet-time idea that will be guaranteed to cheer up someone else would be to take a small gift (basket of muffins, box of candy, a gift certificate for lunch) and go early to a Sunday-school class or the nursery and leave the gift and a thank-you note. Then pray for the ministry that will happen in that room.

For a different approach, on your way to church stop by your local donut shop to read your Bible or engage in conversation with people who are seeking Jesus. Your faith might be refreshed by being a pastor to people who'd never darken the door of a church.

Go on a God Hunt

Our family practices the "God hunt" that we learned from David and Karen Mains on *Chapel of the Air.* On the way to church we pray that God would meet us and help us minister to another. "Bless me and make me a blessing," we pray. Then on the way home we ask: "How did God meet you? How did God use you to encourage someone else?" My sons have never had bad attitudes about going to church, in part I think, because each Sunday we go on a God hunt. We are always looking for the surprises God has for each of us.

From the Pulpit to Your Quiet Time

Sermons can become a springboard for personal devotions. Try reading ahead so you know what territory your pastor might be covering. Trying to second guess or correct your pastor should not be the goal. Use this time to prepare your mind and heart to receive the message. If your pastor is teaching through one of Paul's epistles, you might want to spend your quiet times in Acts so you understand the historical events that Paul is discussing. If the pastor's tackling an Old Testament passage, you might try to find out if the New Testament ever cross-references the topics or verses.

Here are some other ideas for incorporating your church life into your quiet times.

☐ Use sermon notes for quiet times to review how God might want you to apply the sermon to your everyday life.

☐ During the sermon write down questions about topics you'd like to learn more about or thoughts you'd like to consider in a deeper manner at a later quiet time.

☐ Use the prayer list during quiet times to pray for others in your church. Or pray through the church's calendar.

☐ Use traditional liturgies and prayers from your church services in your quiet times.

☐ Have a personal communion service and rewalk the steps of Christ to the cross as you read through Psalm 22 or Matthew 27.

☐ Have a sabbath dinner by candlelight or incorporate other early church traditions to bring an attitude of rest to your Sundays.

Allow Jesus to pastor you each Sunday as you connect to him.

30.

MARKERS

From childhood Albrecht Dürer wanted to paint. Finally, he left home to study with a great artist. He met a friend who also had this same desire and the two became roommates. Both being poor, they found it difficult to make a living and study at the same time. Albrecht's friend offered to work while Albrecht studied. Then when the paintings began to sell, the friend would have his chance. After much persuasion, Albrecht agreed and painted faithfully while his friend toiled long hours to make a living.

The day came when Albrecht sold a wood-carving and his friend went back to his paints, only to find that the hard work had stiffened and twisted his fingers so that he could no longer paint with skill. When Albrecht learned what had happened to his friend, he was filled with great sorrow. One day returning home unexpectedly, he heard the voice of his friend and saw the gnarled, toil-worn hands folded in prayer before him.

"I can show the world my appreciation by painting his

hands as I see them now, folded in prayer." Durer's grati-
tude was captured in his inspired painting that has become
world famous. (Taken from *The Bible Friend* in *Word Search*,
CD-ROM.) It is a visual marker of God's faithfulness.

Remembering

Joshua understood the need for people to have their
memories stimulated. After years of claiming the land
God had promised Israel, each tribe was given a portion
and sent home to settle it. News came that a few tribes
had erected an altar. They said:

> It is to be a witness between us and you and the genera-
> tions that follow, that we will worship the LORD at his
> sanctuary with our burnt offerings, sacrifices and fellow-
> ship offerings. Then in the future your descendants will
> not be able to say to ours, "You have no share in the
> LORD." (Joshua 22:27)

We can create our own altars, our own tangible re-
membrances of the goodness of God in our lives.

Authors Jim and Sally Conway became engaged under
a beautiful tree. Each anniversary they returned to the
tree. Each of their three daughters had her picture taken
under the tree. And after Sally passed away, Jim returned
to grieve under the tree.

In Oklahoma City right after the devastating bomb
that claimed the lives of 168 people, rescue workers
spray-painted a sign on plywood that read: "Good will
overcome evil." The plywood sign was only temporary,
however. It has now been replaced with a beautiful white
marble statue of Christ with his head bowed in mourn-

ing. At his feet is a small plaque with the inscription, "And Jesus wept. John 10:35." The citizens of Oklahoma need that remembrance, as does the rest of the world, that through the compassion and power of God, *good will overcome evil.*

Here are some ways we can create markers.

☐ Consider yearly traditions like writing a Christmas or Thanksgiving poem. Each year on my wedding anniversary I write a poem in my quiet time, thanking God for another good year with my good man.

☐ Make a heirloom gift such as a quilt, cross-stitched picture or pass on a piece of furniture to commemorate an event and hand down faith from generation to generation.

☐ Plant a tree at the birth of our children or at the death of a loved one.

☐ Create a tangible marker like a fountain or a verse etched in wet cement. While at a retreat grounds I walked down a sidewalk of remembrance. Every few steps, a marble plaque was inlaid in the sidewalk with a person's favorite verse. These verses may have been ones they leaned on it times of trouble, believed in for a big transition or founded their marriage on. I'm sure each has a story.

How about you? What can you make that could become a remembrance of your walk with Christ?

For information on Pam Farrel's other books and resources or to contact her write: Masterful Living, 629 S. Rancho Santa Fe, #306, San Marcos, CA 92069. (760) 727-9122. E-mail: mliving@webcc.com